T0009005

CONTENTS

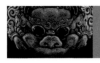

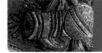

Welcome to the Royal Armouries

We are guardians of the UK's national collection of arms and armour, including the national artillery and national firearms collections. We hold one of the largest collections of historic arms and armour in the world.

The Royal Armouries began life as the main royal and national arsenal housed in the Tower of London. Since the eleventh century, we have occupied buildings within the Tower for making and storing arms, armour and military equipment. In the 1990s, the majority of the collection was moved from London to our purpose-built museum in Leeds.

Royal Armouries Leeds was expressly designed for the arms and armour it holds: even the ceiling heights were calculated to accommodate the longest staff weapons in the collection! The five main galleries house 4,500 objects in the permanent displays.

Your visit will also include the Hall of Steel, a soaring staircase whose walls display historical trophies reminiscent of those erected in the Tower of London after Charles II's restoration in 1660. Outside the museum building itself is a tiltyard where we hold our world-renowned Easter joust, as well as occasional displays of falconry and other forms of mounted martial sport.

We hope you enjoy your visit to Royal Armouries Leeds, and look forward to welcoming you back.

Armour for man and horse

Austrian (Innsbruck) and German, composite, late 15th century

1 **War Gallery, Floor 2**

Gothic armours, fashionable in Germany in the late 15th century, are usually regarded as the pinnacle of the medieval armourer's art. Slender and elegant, with attractive fluted decoration and cusped and scalloped edges, they represent the armourer's version of contemporary Gothic architecture.

Most, like this example, are 'composite', that is, put together from disparate pieces of armour mounted together to make a complete armour.

However, the horse armour of this example is a rarity, being one of only five original medieval German examples in existence. The armour was probably made for Waldemar VI, Prince of Anhalt-Köthen in central Germany. II.3, III.69, 70, 1216, 1300. VI.148, 230, 366, 379, VIII.9, XXI.31

'Danzig' handgun and Longbow

Handgun, Baltic Europe, about 1400. Longbow, English, about 1545

2 **War Gallery, Floor 2**

By the mid 15th century almost all battles involved the use of hand-held firearms. A medieval bronze handgun such as this could penetrate up to 5 mm of sheet steel at short range.

This yew longbow is one of eight recovered in 1840 from the wreck of Henry VIII's warship, the *Mary Rose*, which sank in 1545. As no medieval warbows are known to survive, it is a vital link to the weapons famously used at the battles of Crécy (1346) and Agincourt (1415) where trained bowmen fired 10-12 war arrows a minute over a distance of 229 m (250 yds). XI.103, XII.11833

Writhen Hilt Sword

German, about 1480

❸ War Gallery, Floor 2

This German sword, made in about 1480, was acquired by American media magnate William Randolph Hearst. It has an organic, natural quality that sets it apart from many utilitarian weapons of the fifteenth century. The hilt is made from wood that has been carved to resemble a gnarled stave that flows into a gilt bronze pommel and quillons. A similar sword is wielded by St Michael on a choir screen in Ranworth Church, Norfolk. IX.949

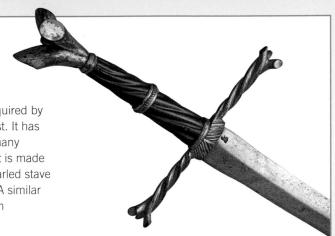

Harquebusier armour of Colonel Alexander Popham

English, about 1630

❹ War Gallery, Floor 2

This rare light armour is traditionally associated with Alexander Popham, a colonel in the army of Parliament during the English Civil Wars. These pieces were originally displayed together in the Great Hall of Littlecote House, Wiltshire. The Littlecote Armoury was rescued for the nation in 1985 following a fundraising effort that included a sponsored march in genuine armour from Wiltshire to London.

In the 17th century, buff leather coats became increasingly common as plate armour fell out of use. The heavy breast and back plates are designed to be shot-proof, with the sharply-angled waistline reflecting the fashion of the period.

III.1956a, III.1957, III.1958, IX.2785

Prototype Maxim machine gun

British, 1884

5 **War Gallery, Floor 3**

This revolutionary weapon was invented by Sir Hiram Maxim in 1884, and is the ancestor of all automatic firearms. It used the recoil of the fired cartridge to operate continuously without manual cranking or re-cocking. This example is the earliest surviving prototype. It is chambered for the .450 cartridge designed for the earlier Gardner and Gatling guns. At more than 40 kg (88 lb), it was extremely heavy. By 1887, Maxim perfected his design and warfare was permanently changed. PR.10510

Thompson Model 1921 submachine gun

American, 1921

6 **War Gallery, Floor 3**

During the First World War, the American Colonel John T. Thompson sought to invent a 'submachine gun' that would serve as a 'trench broom' to 'sweep' the enemy from the trenches. Thompson's prototype was delayed until 1919 by his service in the US Army and no peacetime government wished to purchase it. Instead it appealed to those on the other side of the law: his first customer was the Irish Republican Army. This piece is one of 500 Thompsons smuggled into Ireland in 1921. PR.7398

The 'Horned Helmet'

Austrian, 1511–14

7 **Tournament Gallery, Floor 2**

Made by one of the finest armourers of the age, the 'Horned Helmet' was presented to Henry VIII in 1514 by the Holy Roman Emperor Maximilian I. The remarkable mask (the symbol of the Royal Armouries in Leeds) has a stubbly chin, a pair of spectacles, a hooked nose and an extraordinary pair of ram's horns. It clearly made a powerful impression on Henry, who swiftly established his own royal workshop at Greenwich to match the standard of the emperor's armoury. IV.22

Henry VIII foot combat armour

English, 1520

8 **Tournament Gallery, Floor 2**

This extraordinary foot combat armour is probably the earliest surviving creation of Henry's royal armoury. It was designed for the grand tournament known as the Field of Cloth of Gold (1520), the single largest and most expensive summit-meeting-cum-sporting-event of the sixteenth century, staged just south of Calais between Henry VIII and the French king, Francis I. The armour design was highly fashionable and shows to perfection the tall, muscular figure of the 29-year old English king. II.6

Tilting lances

English, first half of the 16th century

9 Tournament Gallery, Floor 2

A tournament participant would joust over a tilt barrier, scoring points by breaking his lance into three pieces against his opponent's helm. These lances, which probably belonged to Henry VIII, were originally decorated with bright, floral patterns and gilding. They are far too cumbersome for use in a joust, and were probably processional lances, which may explain their unusual survival. VII.551, VII.634

High saddle

German, 1400-15

10 Tournament Gallery, Floor 2

This unusual treasure is the oldest surviving medieval tournament saddle. It is made of wood and covered with rawhide. The first saddles designed exclusively for tournament appeared at the beginning of the 14th century, and differed from war saddles by having long cantle sides enclosing the hips. This saddle is an extreme version; it lifted the jouster thirty centimetres above the horse's back. VI.94

The Lion Armour

Italian or French, 1545-55

11 Tournament Gallery, Floor 3

This armour was probably made for Henry II of France, perhaps inspired by a similar one made for his father, Francis I. The damascened and embossed lion's head decoration is characteristic of the mid-16th century Negroli armourers. During the late 18th century this armour was exhibited as King Charles II in the Tower of London display known as the "Line of Kings". An open-faced helmet, or burgonet, matching this armour has disappeared without trace but is known from a drawing in the Royal Armouries collection. II.89

Elephant armour and tusk swords

Indian, about 1600

12 **Oriental Gallery, Floor 4**

War elephants often formed the shock troops of South
Asian armies. During battles, they were both powerful
fighting animals and intimidating mobile vantage points.
Accounts from the 15th and 16th centuries mention
charging war elephants wearing tusk
swords whilst ravaging enemies on the
battlefield or battering fort defences.
This is the only example of an almost
complete, all-metal elephant armour
in any public collection in the world.
It was probably made in an Indian
arsenal in the late 16th or 17th
century. XXVIA.102 a-f, XXVIA.16, 23, 259,
XXVIL.218, XXVIM.6, AL.290 105, tusk swords
XXVIM.40 A-B

Sword (*jian*)

Chinese, about 1420, Ming Dynasty (1368 – 1644)

⑬ Oriental Gallery, Floor 4

This sword is one of the most beautiful surviving examples of ornate metalwork from the early Ming dynasty. Its decoration is similar to that of several ritual objects known to have been commissioned during the rule of the Yongle Emperor (1403-24). Interaction with Tibetan Buddhism increased in China during this period: as well as the monster mask with its flaming mane and huge jaws, and the intricate dragons curled within cartouches, the sword fittings depict auspicious emblems of Buddhism. This high-status sword could have been made for presentation to a powerful Tibetan monastery or allied ruler, or even for the Yongle Emperor himself. xxvis.295

Mamluk hand cannon (*midfa*)

Syrian, late 15th century

⑭ Oriental Gallery, Floor 4

This bronze bombard is the only known surviving example of a Mamluk hand cannon. The inscription on the breech declares that it was produced on the orders of Emir Kertbey al-Ahmar, Viceroy of Syria during the reign of the Mamluk Sultan al-Nasir Muhammad (1497-98). Emir Kertbey tried to modernise the Mamluk army by establishing four firearms battalions in Damascus, much to the dismay of Mamluk noblemen who jealously guarded their superior status as elite horsemen and archers. xxvif.245

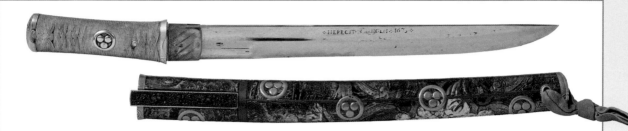

Dagger without hand guard (*aikuchi*)

German blade, 1625, Japanese mounts,
Edo period (1603 – 1867)

15 Oriental Gallery, Floor 4

After the first arrival of Europeans in Japan in 1543, Japanese arms and armour began to incorporate different influences. The Japanese originally thought that European swords were rather primitive, but this dirk incorporates a blade manufactured in Solingen in Germany, reshaped and hardened in the Japanese style. It seems to be the only known Japanese sword in the world fitted with such a blade. The scabbard is covered with painted Dutch leather, used in Europe for covering walls and furniture. XXVID.190

Heavy cavalryman from the Mughal era

Indian, probably early 17th century

16 Oriental Gallery, Floor 4

During the expansion of the Mughal empire (16th-18th centuries), heavy cavalry across northern India and much of the Deccan wore mail and plate armour with helmets. Their horses were also protected by body armour called *bargustawan*. The troops used various combinations of weapons, including the sword, composite bow, lance, mace and saddle axe. They also carried cane shields. Surviving horse armour from this period in South Asian history is extremely rare, especially in near-complete condition. XXVIA.203, 258, XXVIH.18a-c, 27, 28

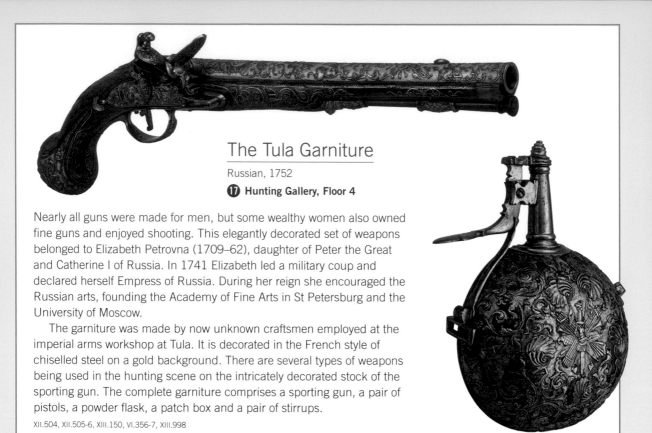

The Tula Garniture

Russian, 1752

17 Hunting Gallery, Floor 4

Nearly all guns were made for men, but some wealthy women also owned fine guns and enjoyed shooting. This elegantly decorated set of weapons belonged to Elizabeth Petrovna (1709–62), daughter of Peter the Great and Catherine I of Russia. In 1741 Elizabeth led a military coup and declared herself Empress of Russia. During her reign she encouraged the Russian arts, founding the Academy of Fine Arts in St Petersburg and the University of Moscow.

The garniture was made by now unknown craftsmen employed at the imperial arms workshop at Tula. It is decorated in the French style of chiselled steel on a gold background. There are several types of weapons being used in the hunting scene on the intricately decorated stock of the sporting gun. The complete garniture comprises a sporting gun, a pair of pistols, a powder flask, a patch box and a pair of stirrups.

XII.504, XII.505-6, XIII.150, VI.356-7, XIII.998

Whaling cannon and grenade harpoon

Norwegian, 1947

18 Hunting Gallery, Floor 4

Originally designed in 1864 by Norwegian whaling entrepreneur Svend Foyn on ideas developed by polar captain Erik Erikson to hunt baleen and blue whales, this cannon was made in 1947 by Kongsberg Vapenfabrikk. Intended to be mounted in the bows, it is a breech-loading 90 mm cannon that fires 51 kg explosive-headed harpoons, or grenades. Similar cannon are used today, particularly by the Icelandic whaling fleet, to hunt minkie whales. Its appearance as a Royal Armouries treasure demonstrates the way in which the collection prompts unexpected questions. XIX.917

Centrefire double-barrelled rifle

English, 1887

⑲ Hunting Gallery, Floor 4

This rare 4-bore rifle played its part in an international love story. 21-year-old Ewart S. Grogan carried it on an epic safari from the Cape to Cairo in 1897, seeking the blessing of his future father-in-law as he pursued his quest to marry New Zealand heiress Gertrude Watt. Such large weapons are often called elephant guns, although Grogan also used the rifle against other big game. XII.3420

Boar sword

Probably German, about 1550

⑳ Hunting Gallery, Floor 4

Boar hunting required particular courage, and dedicated weapons were designed for this dangerous sport. Used purely for thrusting, the blunted blade is strong enough to withstand the considerable force of a charging boar. The cross-piece near the tip – a modern replacement – was necessary because too deep a penetration of the blade would bring the bearer dangerously close to the wounded animal. IX.5391

Hunting spear

French or Italian, about 1600

㉑ Hunting Gallery, Floor 4

Despite the dramatic reduction of forests for agriculture, boar hunting was popular in the 17th century. This exceptional hunting spear is encrusted with gold and silver on a blackened background that depicts trophies of arms, crossed palms, strapwork and stars. It is in the style of Gasparo Mola (1567-1640), a goldsmith who spent much of his life working for the Medici family of Florence. VII.81

Crossbow of 'Balestrino' type

Italian, 17th century

㉒ Self Defence Gallery, Floor 4

Only fifteen of these so-called 'assassins' crossbows are known. Small enough to be concealed by would-be assassins, the hollow handle contains the screw-jack mechanism by which the string is spanned. They clearly posed a tangible threat: in sixteenth-century Venice, the punishment for carrying such a crossbow whilst wearing a mask was to have both hands cut off. In 1594 an assassination plot against Queen Elizabeth I was thwarted in which 'a little cross-bow of steel' was to be used. XI.286

Sword and Buckler

Sword, hilt English, blade possibly German, about 1540 and buckler, probably Welsh, about 1520-45

㉓ Self Defence Gallery, Floor 4

A buckler is a small shield held in the fist, usually used in conjunction with a sword. Made in Wrexham in Wales, they were used widely by infantrymen and civilians from 1440 to 1580. The accompanying sword is one of the best-preserved examples from the reign of Henry VIII. It was discovered in 1979 in the River Thames in London. The remains of a very similar hilt were found on the wreck of the *Mary Rose* which sank in 1545. V.21, IX.4427

Colt 1861 'Navy' model percussion revolvers

American, 1863

24 **Self Defence Gallery, Floor 5**

Symbol of a transatlantic relationship that helped to shape the nineteenth century, this pair of Colt revolvers was presented to Sheffield industrialist Mark Firth. Although they represent early efforts at mass production, the .36 calibre (9 mm) revolvers have been hand-finished to the highest standard. Engraved on the cylinders are scenes from a naval battle of 1843 in which the Texas Commodore Edwin W. Moore defeated a superior fleet of Mexican warships – a crucial event during the young Texas Republic's struggle for independence. PR.3536, PR.3537

M41A Pulse rifle

American, 2170

25 **Self Defence Gallery, Floor 4**

One of the most iconic sci-fi weapons of all time, the 'pulse rifle' was designed by director James Cameron for his classic 1986 film *Aliens*. The firing props combine a Thompson submachine gun from the Second World War with parts from Remington and Franchi shotguns. A custom shell completes the look. This example appeared on screen in both *Aliens* and *Aliens 3* (1992). XII.11846

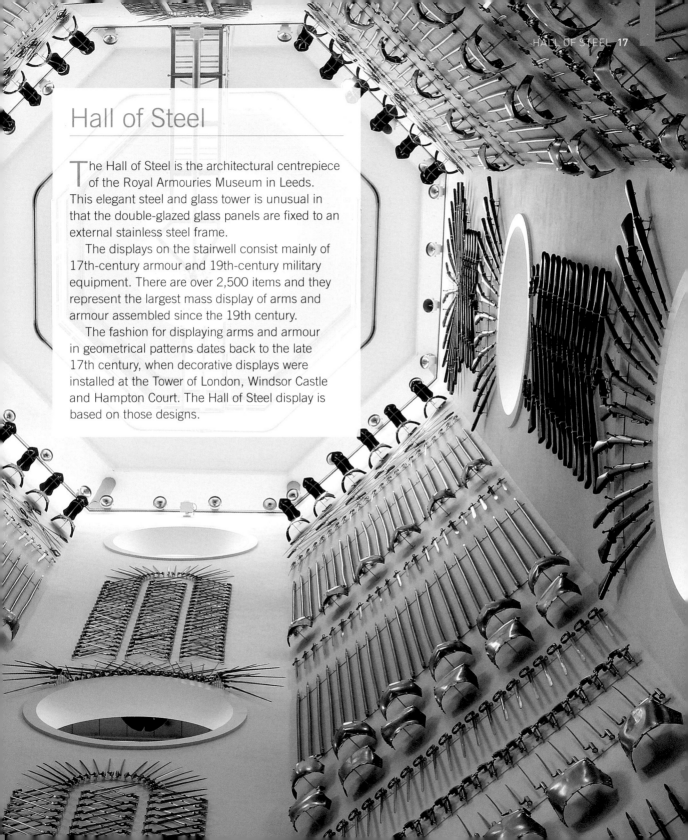

Hall of Steel

The Hall of Steel is the architectural centrepiece of the Royal Armouries Museum in Leeds. This elegant steel and glass tower is unusual in that the double-glazed glass panels are fixed to an external stainless steel frame.

The displays on the stairwell consist mainly of 17th-century armour and 19th-century military equipment. There are over 2,500 items and they represent the largest mass display of arms and armour assembled since the 19th century.

The fashion for displaying arms and armour in geometrical patterns dates back to the late 17th century, when decorative displays were installed at the Tower of London, Windsor Castle and Hampton Court. The Hall of Steel display is based on those designs.

In our largest gallery you can trace the changing face of battle from the days of bloody hand-to-hand combat to today's technology-based warfare. The gallery displays are arranged loosely in chronological order and explore the development of arms and armour from their earliest use to conflicts within living memory.

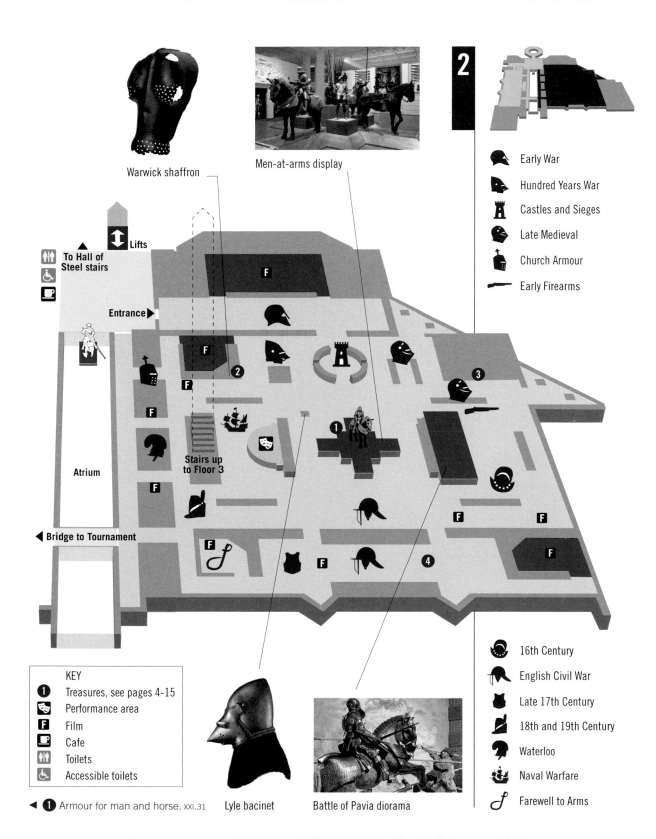

Warwick shaffron

Men-at-arms display

2

Early War

Hundred Years War

Castles and Sieges

Late Medieval

Church Armour

Early Firearms

Lifts

To Hall of
Steel stairs

Entrance ▶

Atrium

Stairs up
to Floor 3

◀ Bridge to Tournament

KEY
1 Treasures, see pages 4–15
Performance area
F Film
Cafe
Toilets
Accessible toilets

16th Century

English Civil War

Late 17th Century

18th and 19th Century

Waterloo

Naval Warfare

Farewell to Arms

◀ 1 Armour for man and horse. xxi.31   Lyle bacinet   Battle of Pavia diorama

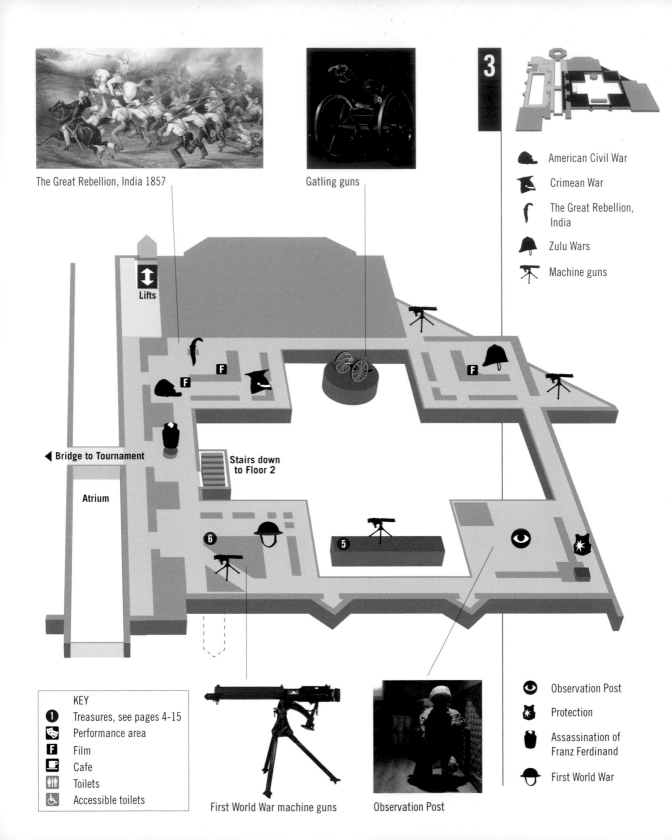

The Great Rebellion, India 1857

Gatling guns

3

- American Civil War
- Crimean War
- The Great Rebellion, India
- Zulu Wars
- Machine guns

Lifts

◀ Bridge to Tournament

Atrium

Stairs down to Floor 2

F

F

F

6

5

- Observation Post
- Protection
- Assassination of Franz Ferdinand
- First World War

KEY
- ❶ Treasures, see pages 4-15
- 🎭 Performance area
- 🇫 Film
- ☕ Cafe
- 🚻 Toilets
- ♿ Accessible toilets

First World War machine guns

Observation Post

Throughout history fighting men have tried to protect themselves from the effects of weapons in battle; at first using animal hides, leather and bone, then bronze, steel and now modern fabrics such as Kevlar. Body protection was adapted in response to weapons development – a momentum continued by the ongoing threat of conflict.

Before the introduction of gunpowder, weapons could only be used for cutting, piercing or crushing at close range. With the arrival of gunpowder weapons were created that used its explosive power to fire bullets or cannon balls much further.

Early War

The story of the War Gallery begins in the ancient world. When you walk into the gallery you will see Neolithic stone weapons, flint hand axes and exquisitely-preserved Bronze Age swords and spearheads. Objects from the Greco-Roman period demonstrate the nature of ancient warfare and the arms and armour that would have been used at such legendary battles as Marathon and Thermopylae. This is the age of Achilles, Alexander the Great, Hannibal and Julius Caesar. It saw the dawn of democracy and the flourishing of one of the greatest empires in history.

▲ Bronze Corinthian helmet, about 650 BC. IV.541

◄ The main weapon of Greek infantry hoplites was a long thrusting spear with an iron head on a 3-metre long wooden haft.

Roman armies

Roman armies were made up of legions. A legion consisted of 5-6,000 foot-soldiers and cavalrymen, uniformly equipped and trained.

The Roman sword (*gladius*) was a short, straight two-edged thrusting sword. The shield (*scutum*) was a hand-held barrier to deflect blows.

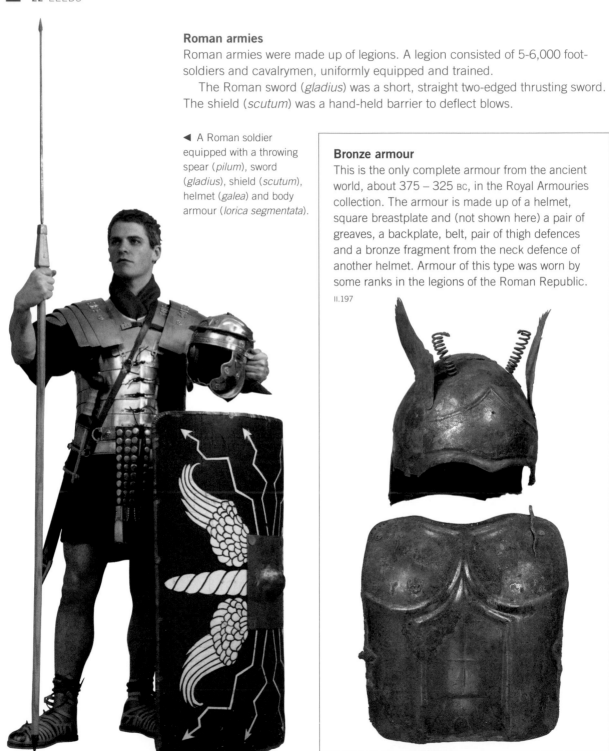

◄ A Roman soldier equipped with a throwing spear (*pilum*), sword (*gladius*), shield (*scutum*), helmet (*galea*) and body armour (*lorica segmentata*).

Bronze armour

This is the only complete armour from the ancient world, about 375 – 325 BC, in the Royal Armouries collection. The armour is made up of a helmet, square breastplate and (not shown here) a pair of greaves, a backplate, belt, pair of thigh defences and a bronze fragment from the neck defence of another helmet. Armour of this type was worn by some ranks in the legions of the Roman Republic.

II.197

The Middle Ages

The Middle Ages typically (albeit contentiously) covers the centuries after the Romans departed Britain until the fall of the Plantagenet dynasty in the 1480s. During this time, there were few standing armies in Europe. Well-armed noblemen and their households formed the core of a country's military strength, supported by temporary troops and paid mercenaries. Many were responsible for training and equipping themselves.

Early Medieval

The breakdown of Roman control across the continent led to the large-scale movement of tribes who flooded Western Europe – the Goths, Vandals, Angles, Saxons and Danes. What we know of their spears, shields, swords and helmets comes mostly from archaeological excavations of burial sites. The infantry of these armies fought in dense and ordered formations. By the tenth century, the usual formation was the 'shield wall', a solid defensive line of infantry spearmen, supported by small numbers of light infantry together with cavalry (who usually dismounted for battle).

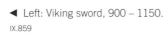

◀ Left: Viking sword, 900 – 1150. IX.859

◀ A throwing axe, of Frankish type, 5th-6th century. VIII.95

▶ The main defensive item of the Anglo-Saxon warrior was the shield. Those who could afford them wore a conical helmet and a mail shirt.

High Medieval

Cavalry

The Normans conquered Anglo-Saxon England in the 11th century. Their military strength came from an initial heavy cavalry charge with lances, and then using swords for close combat. Cavalrymen wore shirts and sometimes leggings of mail, together with a plate iron helmet. They carried a kite-shaped shield.

Mail

The 11th to 13th centuries saw the 'age of mail'. Mail was made of small iron rings riveted together. It was flexible but heavy, with the weight being carried on the shoulders. Mail was not very effective against puncturing weapons such as armour-piercing arrows. Even wearing a quilted linen jacket, or gambeson, beneath the mail could not prevent bruising and broken bones from the force of a blow. The links could be driven into the wound turning it septic.

Plate

In the 13th century, metal plates were riveted to cloth forming a 'pair of plates'. During the following century, which saw the start of the Hundred Years' War between England and France, plates of iron were added to vulnerable points such as elbows and knees for extra protection, and by 1400 knights were fully encased in suits of plate armour that covered most of the body.

◀ Norman cavalryman wearing a mail tunic (hauberk).

▶ 12th-century European sword.
IX.1082

Late Medieval

The late medieval battlefield was dominated by mounted soldiers and men-at-arms. Continual developments in both military tactics and the production of arms and armour saw the use of massed infantry, such as at the battles of Courtrai (1302) and Bannockburn (1314), and more powerful projectile weapons, first in the form of archery and then with the introduction of firepower. By the Wars of the Roses (1455-87), the mounted and armoured man-at-arms not only faced blows from hand-held edged weapons but also from shot fired from handguns.

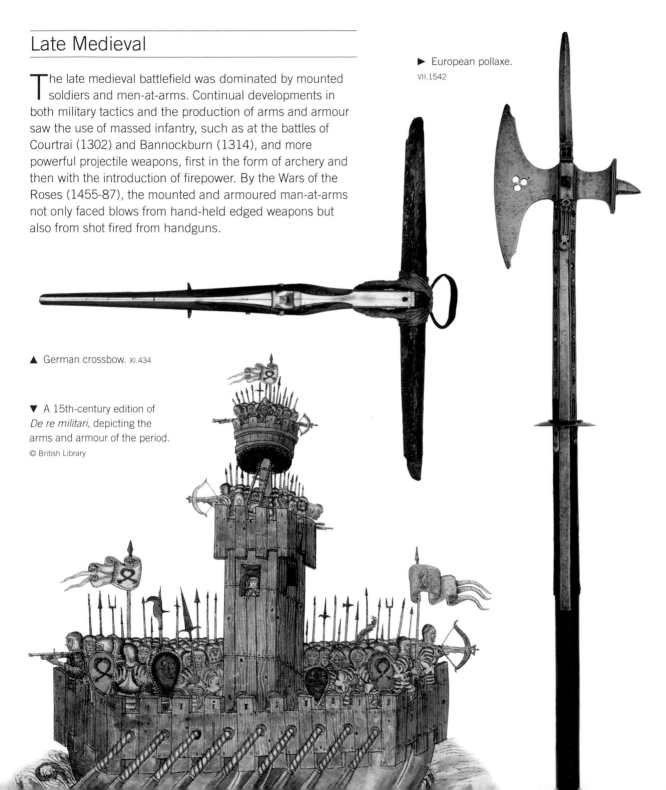

▶ European pollaxe.
VII.1542

▲ German crossbow. XI.434

▼ A 15th-century edition of *De re militari*, depicting the arms and armour of the period.
© British Library

Hundred Years War (1337 – 1453)

The Hundred Years War was a prolonged struggle between the rival kingdoms of England and France.

Rather than being one long war, the Hundred Years War was actually a series of battles on land and sea, sieges, and raids. It grew out of centuries of English-French bickering over the lands which English kings held in France, to which was added in the 1330s an English claim to the French crown itself.

The conflict saw many significant changes in the ways that countries waged war, and the weapons they used. Improvements in infantry training and equipment proved vital. Archers in particular, who had been trained to use their longbows since youth, used their weapons to devastating effect throughout the campaigns.

Technological innovations such as plate armour, early artillery, and the first firearms frequently made the difference between victory and defeat, or life and death.

◄ German long sword. The longer grip and heavier blade enables the sword to be used with two hands to deliver a more powerful blow. IX.915

◄ English 'ballock' dagger. Traditionally sheathed like a sword, the dagger was designed as a close combat weapon. The name is derived from the distinctive shape of the shaft. X.225

The Warwick shaffron

This head defence for a war-horse is the earliest surviving piece of European medieval horse armour as well as an important example from the period of Agincourt. Formed of a main plate and two side plates in steel, it is pierced with large holes for the ears. The eyes are protected by a high embossed plate pierced with holes. VI.446

► German Gothic armour, late 15th century. II.1, III.853, III.1321, IV.499

▲ The Lyle bacinet, late 14th century. One of the finest surviving late medieval bacinets. Commonly called a 'pig-faced' bacinet because of the protruding snout. IV.470

Armour

The 14th century was a period of transition from mail to plate armour. This was in response to developments in infantry weapons such as mail-piercing arrows, which also saw shields gradually become redundant. By 1400 knights wore suits of plate armour that were usually covered by close-fitting coloured coats (jupons). The bottom and rear of the upper legs remained unarmoured so a knight could ride his horse. By the 15th century, it was fashionable to expose the bright metal of the breastplate.

It is tempting to think of the late middle ages as some primitive backwater, whilst instead high-grade weapons technology was being applied and used. As the skills and craftsmanship of armourers did not come cheaply, arms and armour often became symbols of status and power. Consequently, only wealthy knights could afford a full suit of armour, known as a harness, whereas most ordinary soldiers had only a simple breastplate and helmet.

16th Century

By the early 16th century hand-held firearms were being used in battle. They were basic, heavy to carry, slow to load, fired only short distances and were largely inaccurate.

The first battle in which infantry armed with firearms (harquebusiers) were victorious over fully armoured knights took place at Pavia in 1525 between France and the Holy Roman Empire. Metal plate armour proved no defence against bullets.

The invention of firearms did not change battle tactics overnight and for a long time a mixture of weapons was used – swords, pikes, muskets and cannon. By the later years of the 16th century European armies were using more coordinated groups of specialist troops such as musketeers and pikemen.

▼ This form of gun developed early in the 16th century. A light barrel was fitted into a wooden stock which also provided a place of attachment for a simple lock mechanism. (The lock is missing from this gun.) XII.1787

▼ Detail from a contemporary painting of the battle of Pavia, illustrating the arms and armour of the period. I.42

▲ Italian morion. Various types
of brimmed helmets without
face protection were worn by
infantry. IV.1565

▶ Armour of the soldier and
military writer Sir John Smythe
bequeathed to James I in 1607.
Shown with a wheellock pistol.
II.84, XII.716

◀ Left: Italian glaive. VII.944

◀ German halberd. VII.1504

17th Century

The period of the English Civil Wars (1638-53) was important for changes in both arms and armour, as well as the types of soldiers employed in battle. Firearms became more important and armour was used less than before. By the end of the 17th century fixing a stout knife into the muzzle of a musket had produced the first bayonet, and gradually this development replaced the pike which had been a feature of the battlefield for over 200 years.

Foot soldiers

There were two types of infantryman employed during the English Civil Wars, the pikeman and the musketeer.

The pikeman wore a steel breastplate over a woollen jacket. The distinctive pikeman's pot helmet was lined, but it could not stop musket balls.

The bulk of the fighting fell to the musketeers with their relatively long-range weapons rather than to the pikeman, whose effectiveness was limited by the length of his pike. Pikemen were mainly used to protect the musketeers from cavalry charges.

Cavalrymen

In the early 17th century the lancer had been replaced by the cuirassier, wearing three-quarter armour and armed with a pair of pistols and a sword. But the harquebusier, or light cavalryman, was the much more common kind of mounted soldier.

▲ Pikeman's armour. II.365 A-E

▲ Top right: Pikeman from Jacob de Gheyn's book *Wappenhandelinge* (1607).

▲ Wheellock holster pistol. XII.1267

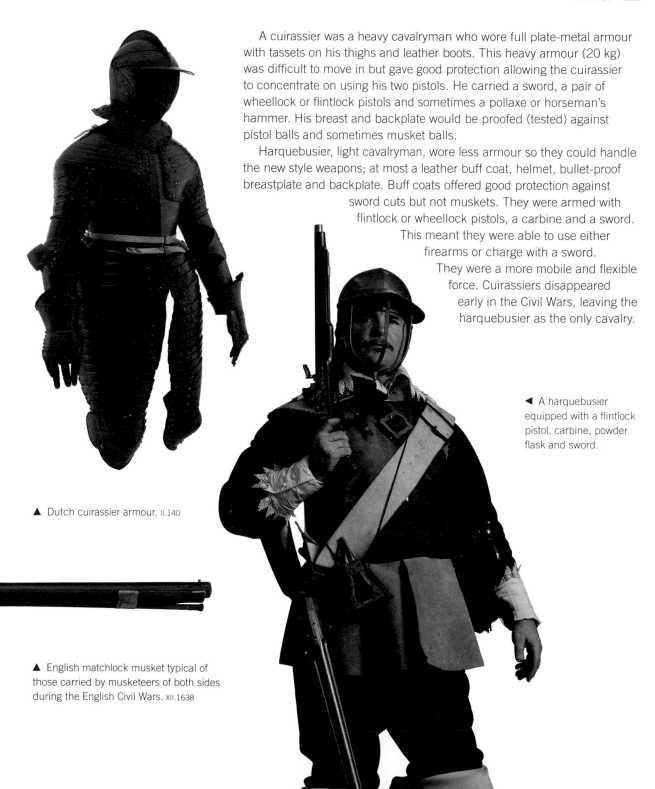

A cuirassier was a heavy cavalryman who wore full plate-metal armour with tassets on his thighs and leather boots. This heavy armour (20 kg) was difficult to move in but gave good protection allowing the cuirassier to concentrate on using his two pistols. He carried a sword, a pair of wheellock or flintlock pistols and sometimes a pollaxe or horseman's hammer. His breast and backplate would be proofed (tested) against pistol balls and sometimes musket balls.

Harquebusier, light cavalryman, wore less armour so they could handle the new style weapons; at most a leather buff coat, helmet, bullet-proof breastplate and backplate. Buff coats offered good protection against sword cuts but not muskets. They were armed with flintlock or wheellock pistols, a carbine and a sword. This meant they were able to use either firearms or charge with a sword. They were a more mobile and flexible force. Cuirassiers disappeared early in the Civil Wars, leaving the harquebusier as the only cavalry.

◀ A harquebusier equipped with a flintlock pistol, carbine, powder flask and sword.

▲ Dutch cuirassier armour. II.140

▲ English matchlock musket typical of those carried by musketeers of both sides during the English Civil Wars. XII.1638

18th and 19th Century

After the 17th century defensive armour virtually disappeared from use, in a response to the development of firearms, as it gave little protection against bullets.

Infantry armed with a musket, which could be fitted with a bayonet and used like a pike once fired, caused changes in battlefield tactics. The 18th century saw the development of 'linear' warfare, the deployment of bodies of infantry in tight formation firing in volleys and then charging with fixed bayonets. Tactics like these were employed during the American War of Independence and most dramatically in Britain's wars with France at the end of the 18th and beginning of the 19th century.

The flintlock musket and socket bayonet of the infantry, and the sword of the cavalry were the dominant weapons at the Battle of Waterloo, 1815. Large numbers of light infantry armed with rifles and French cavalry armed with lances also played a major role in the campaign.

◄ Pattern 1796 Heavy Cavalry trooper's sword. IX.2710

► 'The Battle of Waterloo' from Orme's *Military and Naval Anecdotes* (1819).

▲ Flintlock musket. The last of the flintlocks, the New Land Pattern musket, was introduced around 1802. XII.132

▲ Pattern 1796 Light Cavalry officer's sword. IX.835

Mass production

The early years of the 19th century heralded an industrial age the like of which had never before been witnessed.

Formerly a labour-intensive and expensive industry, by the early 1850s the production of military firearms had become largely mechanised. American manufacturers like Colt and Whitney had shown that it was feasible to use unskilled labour to produce perfectly adequate firearms, with a minimum of skilled workers for hand finishing. British entrepreneurs were not slow to adopt mechanisation and firearms manufacturers such as the London Armoury Company and the Royal Small Arms Manufactory, Enfield all used the latest technology to ensure complete interchangeability of parts, uniform fit and speed of assembly.

Uniforms

The British Army gained its nickname the 'Redcoats' from the colour of the woollen coats the regiments wore. Oliver Cromwell's New Model Army in the 17th century was the first to wear red coats as a uniform.The 18th and 19th century was a time of ornamental military uniforms. By mass-producing uniforms thousands of soldiers could be equipped quickly and the standard sizes and designs were easier to replace on campaign. These colourful uniforms eventually gave way in the late 19th century to khaki tunics more suited for actual combat.

▲ Pattern 1853 Enfield rifled musket. The first rifle to be issued to all line infantry, and the first to be mass-produced, it first saw service in the Crimean War. XII.1914

The First World War

In 1914, for the first time since Napoleon's defeat at Waterloo, all of Europe's great powers faced each other across a shattered peace. The First World War was a watershed in global history, destroying four empires and costing nearly ten million lives.

The war also led to major advances in military strategy and tactics that were reflected in the weapons used on the battlefield. Commanders familiar with fighting colonial battles in the name of empire suddenly faced the extraordinary challenge of warfare on a truly industrial scale, as the improvised nature of trench warfare contrasted with the power of the weaponry ranged against them.

▲ British Brodie Mark I 'B' Pattern helmet. IV.1821

▶ American-made 1917 'Enfield' bolt-action rifle and sword bayonet. Both are copies of the original British Pattern 1913 designs. PR.10501, XII.11670

▲ Lead-cored trench club, with hobnail studs. VIII.55

Vickers-Maxim Mark 1 machine gun
In 1912 the Sheffield-based company Vickers produced a much smaller and lighter version of the Maxim gun, perhaps the definitive Maxim-type machine gun, a model that was much simpler to produce and maintain than Germany's own Maxim MG 08. XII.11295

▲ German *Stahlhelm* in early camouflage finish. IV.1652

Though the human cost was immense, repeated efforts were made by all sides to bring a decisive end to the fighting. Military technology, which in the late 19th century had outpaced strategy and tactical innovation, now developed to reflect the needs of the troops, and different ways were found to deploy the new weaponry. Static warfare also drove the development of bigger and bigger guns. From bolt-action rifles and submachine guns to breech-loading howitzers and quick-firing field guns, these technological changes continue to define modern warfare and influence the range of military equipment in use today.

▲ German Modell 1889 Cavalry sword. The pierced guard includes the crest of the eagle of Prussia. IX.7677

▼ German Bergmann MP 18,1 submachine gun. PR.7355

◄ Men of the Royal Artillery on the Somme with a huge BL 6-inch Mk VII field gun. RAR.0970

This gallery shows some of the fearsome weapons used and the special armours developed for protection in different competitions.

Tournaments were extreme sporting events that were often organised to show royal or noble power. Like modern elite sports events, many tournaments were also lavish displays that brought together competitors and spectators from far and wide.

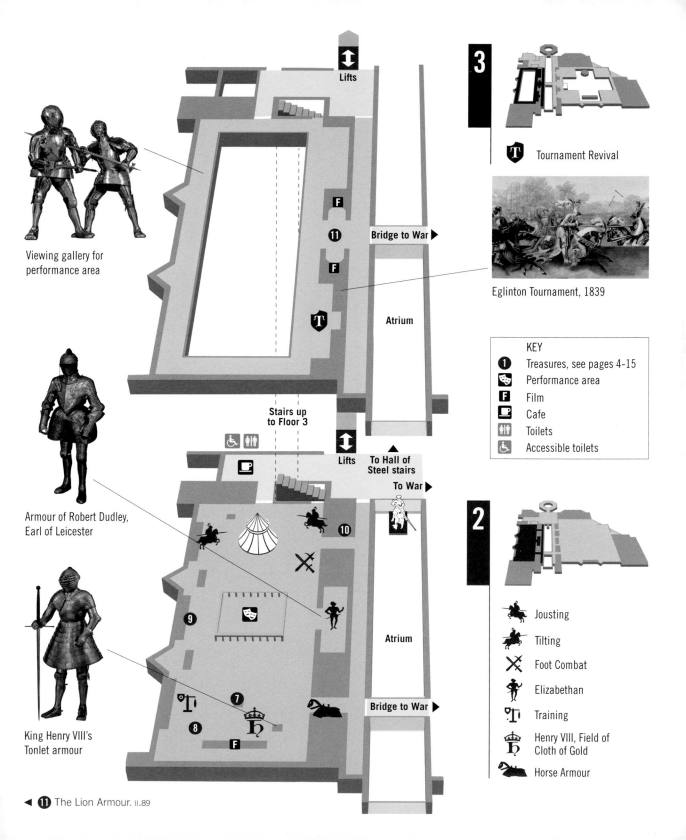

Lifts

Viewing gallery for
performance area

F

11

F

Bridge to War ▶

T

Atrium

3

T Tournament Revival

Eglinton Tournament, 1839

KEY

1 Treasures, see pages 4-15
Performance area
F Film
Cafe
Toilets
Accessible toilets

Armour of Robert Dudley,
Earl of Leicester

Stairs up
to Floor 3

Lifts

To Hall of
Steel stairs

To War ▶

10

Atrium

9

7

T

8

H

F

Bridge to War ▶

King Henry VIII's
Tonlet armour

2

Jousting

Tilting

Foot Combat

Elizabethan

T Training

Henry VIII, Field of
Cloth of Gold

Horse Armour

▲ Tournament parade, from a manuscript account of the jousts between Jehan Chalons of England and 'Loys de Beul' of France at Tours, 1446. I.35

Tournament

Tournaments probably began in the 11th century as mock battles between two opposing teams and provided good training for war. Different forms of combat developed, each with its own type of armour, weapons and rules. Tournaments became spectator events, often with lavish costumes and prizes. As a colourful, chivalrous and dangerous spectacle the tournament lasted 600 years.

There were three forms of tournament combat – tourney, joust and foot combat. Each event had its own set of rules dictating the type of armour and weapons that could be used.

Tourney

Tourneys, especially popular in the 12th century, were fought in teams as mock battles in the countryside. Over time these events were confined to fenced enclosures. Teams fought with blunted lances and swords, wearing battle armour with many extra reinforcing pieces. The aim was to capture an opponent and hold them for ransom not to kill them, although deaths did occur in such a dangerous sport.

Jousting helm

The large slot at the front of this 'frog-mouthed' helm allowed the wearer to take aim by leaning forwards. He then straightened up to protect his eyes from broken lance pieces. This meant that at the moment of impact he could see nothing and could only feel the hit! IV.411

Heraldic Shields

In combat it was hard to identify knights wearing helmets. This meant that their bravery and skill might go unrecognised or that they might be attacked by their own side. Knights used badges so people could see who they were. These were displayed on their helmets, surcoats and shields. Some families developed coats of arms that showed who their parents, grandparents and even great-grandparents were. Many used symbols that were special to their family name or estates.

▶ Illustration showing Ulrich von Liechtenstein with an image of Venus on his helmet. © Universitätsbibliothek Heidelberg

Victorious knights were entitled to seize the horse and armour of those they defeated – good tournament fighters could make their fortunes this way.

Joust

The joust was a contest between two mounted knights charging at each other armed with long wooden lances. By the late 15th century there were two forms of the joust: the *joust of war*, fought with sharp, solid lances with the aim of unhorsing your opponent, and the *joust of peace*, fought with hollow lances with the aim of shattering lances.

Jousting over a barrier was called tilting, the central barrier (the tilt) being introduced to prevent collisions.

Foot combat

Weapons used in this event included spears, maces, pollaxes or two-handed swords. This type of combat was regulated with a set number of blows agreed beforehand and taken alternately by each knight. By the late 16th century bouts were fought over a barrier so there was no need for armour to protect the lower leg.

▶ An interpretation of foot combat with pollaxes.

King Henry VIII

▲ Portrait of Henry VIII, after Holbein, late 16th century. I.51

▼ The Field of Cloth of Gold, artist unknown. The Royal Collection © 2019 HM Queen Elizabeth II

Henry came to the English throne in 1509 at the age of 18. As a young man he excelled at tennis and wrestling and enjoyed skill-at-arms, archery, jousting and foot combat.

Field of Cloth of Gold, June 1520
The accession of François I to the throne of France brought a change to the diplomatic relations between France and England. This new friendship was embodied in the most magnificent tournament ever held, called the Field of Cloth of Gold as the kings' tents were made with cloth of gold.

The two kings met between Calais and Guines, on the border of the English enclave around Calais and French territory, and the festivities lasted for about two weeks. This extravagant and expensive event took months of planning. The tournament culminated in the signing of a peace treaty between the two powers, as well as giving the two young kings ample opportunity to show off their chivalric skills.

King Henry who, at 29 years old and over six feet tall, was a fine athlete, took part in many of the combats. It is said that on one particular day he ran so many courses that his horse died of exhaustion!

❽ Foot combat armour

This armour was in production for Henry VIII to wear at the Field of Cloth of Gold, but was never completed. A change in the rules for the armour worn in the foot combat event occurred and work on this armour ceased. It remained undecorated. II.6

Tonlet armour

The armourers at Greenwich had a very short time to make a new armour for Henry VIII to wear at the Field of Cloth of Gold. They succeeded in preparing this armour, known as the Tonlet armour because of its hooped skirt of that name, by adapting a number of existing pieces and decorating the armour. Only the pauldrons and the tonlet were made new. II.7

Horse armour

▶ Shaffron, 1515-1525. VI.36

One of a knight's most valuable possessions was his best horse and because he owned a 'cheval', or horse, in French he was called a 'chevalier'. A horse needed special protection in tournaments and war.

Horse armour was introduced to protect the horse's head, neck and flanks against blows from lances, swords and, in battle, arrows. Horse armour was first made of textiles or mail. However, from about 1450 steel plate was used.

The Burgundian Bard

This horse armour was a gift from the Holy Roman Emperor Maximilian I to Henry VIII to mark his marriage to Katherine of Aragon in 1509. It is described in an English inventory of 1519 as 'given by the Emperor'.

It is embossed with a trailing design of pomegranates (Katherine's badge) and the firesteels and ragged (raguly) crosses of the Burgundian Order of the Golden Fleece which Henry had been awarded in 1505. VI.6-12

Gloriana: Queen Elizabeth I

Henry VIII was succeeded by his children: Edward, Mary and finally Elizabeth. The salaried armourers at the royal workshop at Greenwich continued to work for the monarch, but Elizabeth, who would not have competed in tournaments, probably never wore armour. She found a profitable way of running the workshop by selling expensive licences to favoured courtiers. The Royal Armouries holds the world's finest collection of these Elizabethan courtiers' armours.

After 1580 Elizabeth's knights held special tournaments on 17 November each year to mark her accession to the throne. These games took place at Whitehall Palace and included poems, speeches and plays praising the queen. However, many of those who placed lavish orders with the royal Greenwich armoury sank deep into debt as they attempted to curry favour with the queen.

▲ An early-18th century portrait of Elizabeth I.

▲ This armet for tilt was made for Sir Henry Lee in the Greenwich royal workshop under master armourer Jacob Halder. Sir Henry Lee was Elizabeth's champion in the 1580s and arranged her Accession Day jousts in the 1590s. IV.43

▶ Armour of Robert Dudley, Earl of Leicester. Configured for the tilt. II.81

This gallery concentrates upon the great civilisations of Asia, and its purpose is to show how arms and armour can provide a key to understanding Asian history.

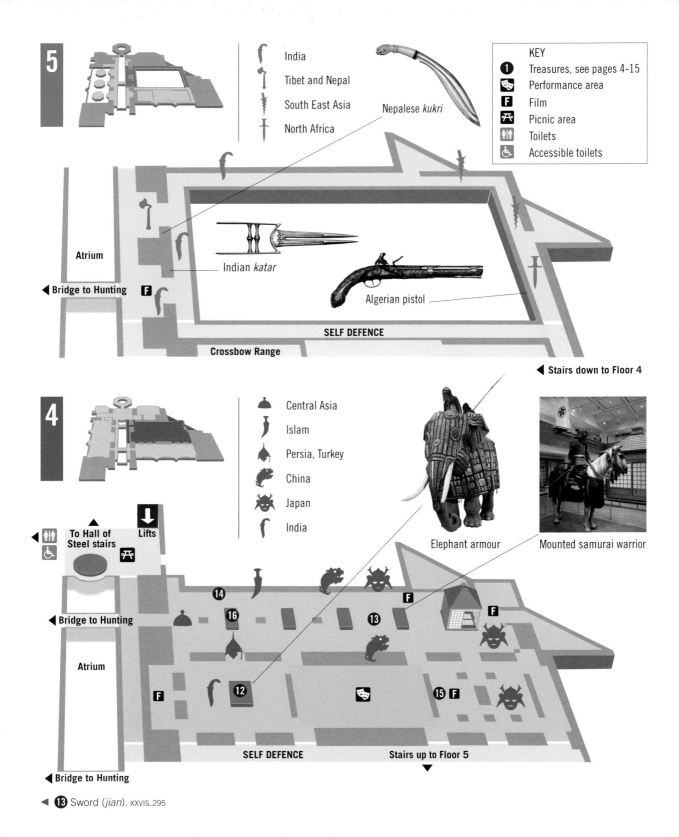

5

India
Tibet and Nepal
South East Asia
North Africa

Nepalese *kukri*

KEY
1 Treasures, see pages 4-15
Performance area
F Film
Picnic area
Toilets
Accessible toilets

Atrium

◀ Bridge to Hunting   F

Indian *katar*

Algerian pistol

SELF DEFENCE

Crossbow Range

◀ Stairs down to Floor 4

4

Central Asia
Islam
Persia, Turkey
China
Japan
India

Elephant armour

Mounted samurai warrior

◀ Toilets
To Hall of Steel stairs   ▼ **Lifts**
Accessible toilets   Picnic

◀ **Bridge to Hunting**

Atrium

14

16

F   12

13   F

F

15   F

SELF DEFENCE   **Stairs up to Floor 5**
▼

◀ **Bridge to Hunting**

◀ **13** Sword (*jian*). XXVIS.295

The cultures of Asia are far more diverse than those of Europe, and the gallery is divided into a number of distinct zones – Central Asia, Turkey, Persia, Islam, the Indian sub-continent, China, Japan and South East Asia. There is one theme that unites all these diverse cultures and has dominated the way in which war was waged in most of them until the 19th century: the use of the mounted archer.

Islam

The rise of Islam

The rise of Islam both as a religion and a world power was an extraordinary phenomenon. The Hijri era, still used throughout the Islamic world, began with the Hijra (flight or migration) of the Prophet Muhammad from Mecca to Medina in 622. Victory at the battle of Badr (624) established Muhammad's ascendancy over western Arabia, and by the time of his death in 632 his authority was supreme in most of Arabia.

▼ The arms and armour of a heavy cavalryman, as used across the Eurasian Steppe for over a thousand years. XXVIA.122, 157, 276, XXVIB.78,141,145, XXVIH.21,22,38, XXVIS.298, AL.189 12-21

Turks and Mongols

The Turkish military system, based on the use of armoured horse archers, was introduced into the Islamic world in the 9th century. They came first as slave soldiers (*ghilman*), but by the 11th century founded their own Muslim dynasties and empires. The central Asian Mongolian tribes, who fought in the same way, conquered most of the established Islamic dynasties in the west under Genghis Khan in the 13th century and China in the east under Kubilai Khan. With the break-up of the great Khanate, however, most of the Mongol successor states also embraced Islam. The most powerful Islamic empire in the west by the 15th century was the Ottoman Turkish empire; the Ottomans captured Constantinople in 1453 using heavy artillery, and built an empire that controlled northern Africa, western Asia and eastern Europe until the mid 19th century.

Africa

The north coast of Africa was added to the emerging Muslim empire in the 7th century and Spain was conquered in the 8th century. Little is known of the arms and armour of Africa before the 19th century when great quantities were brought back to Europe as souvenirs of colonial wars.

Armour

Most of the body defences surviving from Saharan Africa were worn by cavalry. They consist of quilted cotton decorated with coloured panels either worn on their own or with shirts of riveted mail. Many were brought back as trophies after the Omdurman campaign of 1898. The conical helmets were often very old – surviving from the 15th and 16th centuries. The mail worn was often old but riveted mail continued to be made at Omdurman well into the 19th century.

▼ Fabric coat (*jibbah*) and helmet. Sudanese, 19th century. XXVIA.104, 191

▲ Arm knife (*loi-bo*) and scabbard. Somali, late 19th century. XXVID.137

◄ Sword (*cascara*). Sudanese, Darfur, dated 1898-9. This example has a 17th century Italian blade. XXVIS.112

China

M any military inventions came from China, including the crossbow and perhaps most important of all, gunpowder. Chinese arms and armour could also be great works of art.

▶ Repeating crossbow (*zhuge nu*) and set of quarrels, Qing dynasty, 19th century. XXVIB.36 and XXVIB.11 a-j

Crossbow

One of the great innovations in military technology was the development of the crossbow (*nu*) probably in the 4th century BC; in particular the cast bronze crossbow lock mechanism. All excavated examples are from the Han period, 206 BC – AD 220, but the crossbow continued to be an important weapon in China until the 19th century.

▲ Bronze gun, probably Ming dynasty or early Qing dynasty, 15th-17th century. This simple gun has a heavy bronze barrel wrapped in silk and bound with tough lacquered gut or rattan to form carrying handles. XIX.307

Gunpowder weapons

The recipe for gunpowder, mixing saltpetre, sulphur and charcoal was known in China during the Tang dynasty, 7th – 8th centuries AD.

The earliest know metal-barrelled cannon comes from Heilongjian, it was cast in bronze about 1288. The earliest cast-iron cannon is dated 1338. Unlike artillery, hand firearms were a late introduction to China in the middle years of the 16th century.

▲ Matchlock wall gun (*chong*). Qing dynasty, 18th-19th century. XXVIF.44

Lamellar armour

This is typical of the leather lamellar armours of western China. Lamellae are small plates of rawhide, heavily lacquered to protect them from the effects of moisture, the lacing being leather. Some scales are decorated with carving. These may have formed decorative borders to the armour, or may have been incorporated from an earlier coat, when the armour was last re-laced. The helmet is constructed of laced plates and bordered with leopard skin. Similar lamellae have been excavated from 6th-century sites in Chinese Central Asia.

Armour

During the early Ming dynasty (1368–1644), these so-called 'brigandine' armours became the commonest type in China. They consist of a jacket of heavy fabric with separate sleeves, all covered with embroidered silk and lined with numerous, small tinned iron plates fastened by gilt rivets. To this were added ornately shaped shoulder guards, leg defences and originally an iron helmet with a plate-lined fabric neck guard.

◀ Left: Lamellar armour from Sichuan, probably 18th century. XXVIA.106

◀ *Ding jia* armour, probably 17th century. XXVIA.135–6

▼ Armour of butted mail (*zirih*) with a four-plate cuirass (*chahar a'ineh*), helmet (*top*) and armguards (*dastana*), made in Lahore in the early 19th century. XXVIA.6

India

A rms and armour featured as a central part of Indian culture from earliest times. The heroes of early epic stories such as the *Mahabharata* rode on chariots and shoot bows, and archery played a central role in all Indian military systems until the widespread introduction of firearms in the 18th century.

Armour

The earliest forms of armour from India are of scale. Mail and plate armour was probably introduced into India under the Mughals. Coats and helmets were made from small overlapping iron scales connected by rows of mail links. Coats had large plates at the front and quilted linings. Trousers of mail were worn on the legs.

In the late 18th century this type of armour was replaced by four plates joined by straps. This was copied from contemporary Persian armour.

16 **Cavalry**   **12** **War elephants**

Helmet and cuirass

This body armour (*peti*) comprising a helmet and cuirass is made of quilted fabric covered in embroidered velvet. It is associated with the royal arsenal of Tipu Sultan, ruler of the southern Indian state of Mysore from 1782–99. An ally of France, he was defeated by the forces of the East India Company at the siege of his capital, Seringapatam in 1799.
XXVIA.139

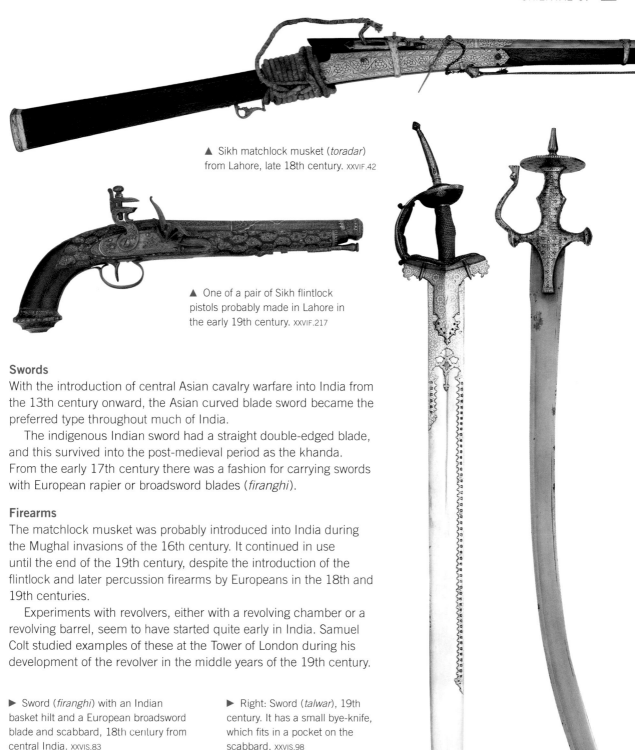

▲ Sikh matchlock musket (*toradar*) from Lahore, late 18th century. xxviF.42

▲ One of a pair of Sikh flintlock pistols probably made in Lahore in the early 19th century. xxviF.217

Swords

With the introduction of central Asian cavalry warfare into India from the 13th century onward, the Asian curved blade sword became the preferred type throughout much of India.

The indigenous Indian sword had a straight double-edged blade, and this survived into the post-medieval period as the khanda. From the early 17th century there was a fashion for carrying swords with European rapier or broadsword blades (*firanghi*).

Firearms

The matchlock musket was probably introduced into India during the Mughal invasions of the 16th century. It continued in use until the end of the 19th century, despite the introduction of the flintlock and later percussion firearms by Europeans in the 18th and 19th centuries.

Experiments with revolvers, either with a revolving chamber or a revolving barrel, seem to have started quite early in India. Samuel Colt studied examples of these at the Tower of London during his development of the revolver in the middle years of the 19th century.

▶ Sword (*firanghi*) with an Indian basket hilt and a European broadsword blade and scabbard, 18th century from central India. xxvis.83

▶ Right: Sword (*talwar*), 19th century. It has a small bye-knife, which fits in a pocket on the scabbard. xxvis.98

Japan

Much of Japan's early culture was imported via Korea from the great civilisation of Tang dynasty China (608–907). Chinese characters, which are the basis of Japanese writing, and a great deal of the social structure were imported. All the armour and weaponry associated with the medieval samurai have their origins on mainland Asia at this time.

The Japanese sword

The Japanese sword is unique in the world in its cultural status. It is one of the divine objects of the Shinto religion, incorporating air, earth, fire and water in its production.

It acquired a shape and method of construction around AD 1000 that later swordsmiths were unable to improve upon. The long sword became a symbol of rank for the military class, the *buke*. Famous artists were employed to design the sword's furniture (fittings) and the most skilled craftsmen to translate these designs into metal.

Historical swords and armours are much more highly regarded in Japan than elsewhere because of the Shinto association of these objects with the spirits of the dead.

Samurai

The ancient Japanese warrior class is known as the *bushi* or samurai. The samurai had rights and privileges, but also obligations – including the requirement to fight for and give complete loyalty to his feudal master. From 1192, when Minamoto Yoritomo was named Shogun, to the restoration of the Meiji Emperor to political power in 1868, the samurai class effectively ruled Japan. The lesser samurai owed allegiance to their feudal lords or *daimyo* ('great names') who formed the land-holding aristocracy.

▶ Equipment of a samurai of the Edo period. XXVIH.42, XXVIA.42, AL.268 5

▼ Armour (*tosei gusoku*) laced with blue silk, made for a member of the Sakakibara family, 16th century. XXVIA.274

▲ Top: Short sword (*wakizashi*), mid 17th century. XXVIS.198

▲ Matchlock musket (*teppo*), early 19th century. XXVIF.52

Firearms

Firearms were introduced to Japan by Portuguese traders in 1543 and forward-thinking commanders began to equip their low-ranking soldiers with them. As in Europe, the finest swordsmen could be defeated by a peasant armed with a gun after only a few hours training. Old-style lamellar armour was virtually useless against bullets; simple armours of plate began to appear on the battlefield.

Lamellar armour

Early Japanese armours were lamellar, that is, the major components were made up from lamellae, small scales of iron or rawhide called *sane*. The armour was elegant, efficient against arrows, spears and swords but was very delicate and easily damaged. The silk laces soaked up moisture and eventually needed replacing. The armour was also prone to become infested with lice and fleas.

During the 16th century the increase in the scale of conflict and the quantity of armour needed in the civil wars, as well as the lengthening of the campaigning season, led armourers to simplify the armour they made. Instead of forming elements from the traditional lamellae, they used solid plates, often lacquered to simulate lamellae. The lacing was simplified so it was easier to keep clean and much quicker to make. Helmets were simplified too: the multi-plate types of the Middle Ages gave way to simple three- or five-plate types. These were often decorated with elaborate crests formed of papier-mâché and lacquered.

South and South East Asia

The hill peoples of central India

The hills and jungles, which separate the Indus-Ganges Plain in the north from the Deccan and the south of India, were a significant barrier to military and political expansion. In consequence weapons closely related to those of antiquity survived almost to the present day among these isolated communities.

The arms of Sri Lanka

Sri Lanka developed distinctive weapons including the dagger (*piha kaetta*) and the sword (*kastane*).

Malaya and Indonesia

The national weapon of Malaya and Indonesia is the *kris*. The kris is traditionally made of a mixture of meteoric iron and steel; the characteristic pattern, which looks like water, on the blade is produced by corroding the metal with a mixture of lime juice and arsenic. The *kris* was carried by all adult males, tucked into the back of the sarong at the waist.

The Philippines

The armour developed by the Moro people of the Philippines is unique. It is of mail and plate construction, the plates being of horn and the mail of brass, a style clearly influenced by the armour of the medieval Islamic world. The helmets were also constructed from horn and brass, but in the style of European burgonets of the 16th century, influenced by contact with early Portuguese explorers and traders.

Arms of mainland south-east Asia

In Burma the weapons used were very similar to those of the south-western Chinese peoples. The name of the sword, the *dha*, is linguistically allied to the Chinese *dao*. Crossbows were used extensively in warfare and hunting, and these show a type of lock mechanism far more primitive than those used by the Chinese in the 3rd century BC. Elephants played an important role in warfare as shock troops.

◄ Left: Khond axe *(tongi)*. The principal weapon of the Khond tribes was the two-handed axe. It had a wide variety of often multiple-pointed blades. XXVIC.22

◄ Sri Lankan sword *(kastane)*, blade probably 19th century, hilt early 17th century. XXVIS.167

Arms of Tibet and Nepal

The Central Asian curved sword never became fashionable in Tibet where the long single-edged sword, used until the 10th century by the steppe peoples, survived. In Nepal, on the south side of the Himalayas, very different swords were used. The earlier type is the *kora*, a forward-curved sword, almost always decorated on the wide point of its blade with an eye.

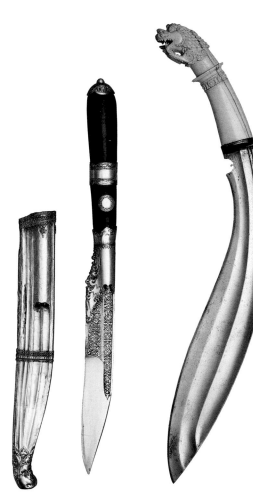

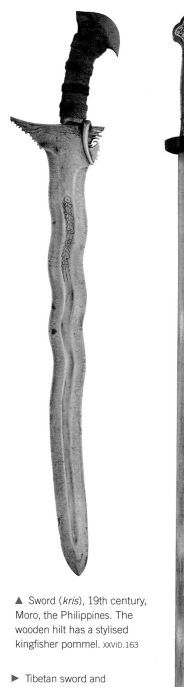

▲ Sword (*kris*), 19th century, Moro, the Philippines. The wooden hilt has a stylised kingfisher pommel. XXVID.163

▲ Sri Lankan dagger (*piha kaetta*) and silver-mounted scabbard, probably 18th century. XXVID.82

▲ A Nepalese *kukri* with an ivory hilt carved in the form of a lion, made in the 19th century. XXVID.30

▶ Tibetan sword and scabbard, 17th–19th century, with silver fittings set with turquoise and coral. XXVIS.187

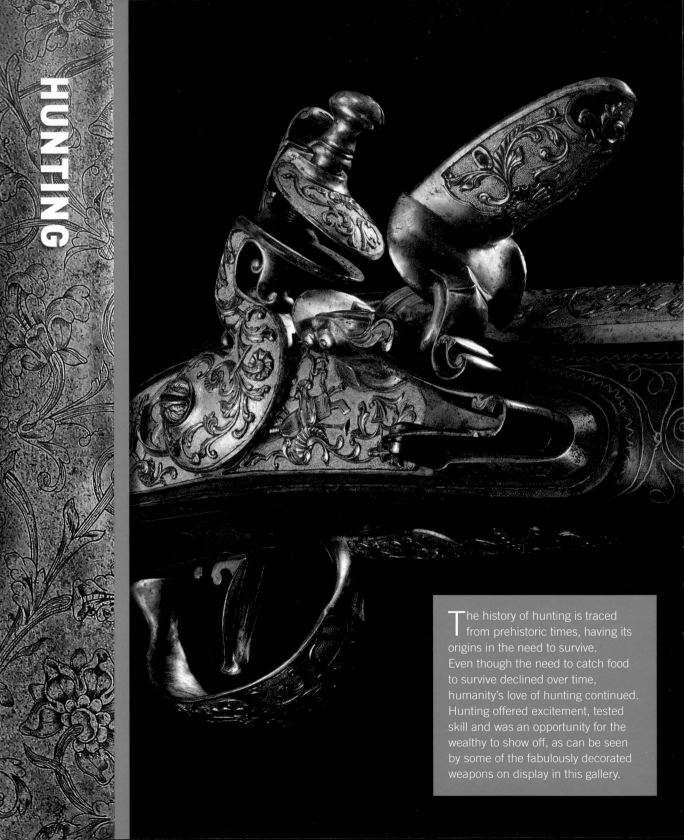

The history of hunting is traced from prehistoric times, having its origins in the need to survive. Even though the need to catch food to survive declined over time, humanity's love of hunting continued. Hunting offered excitement, tested skill and was an opportunity for the wealthy to show off, as can be seen by some of the fabulously decorated weapons on display in this gallery.

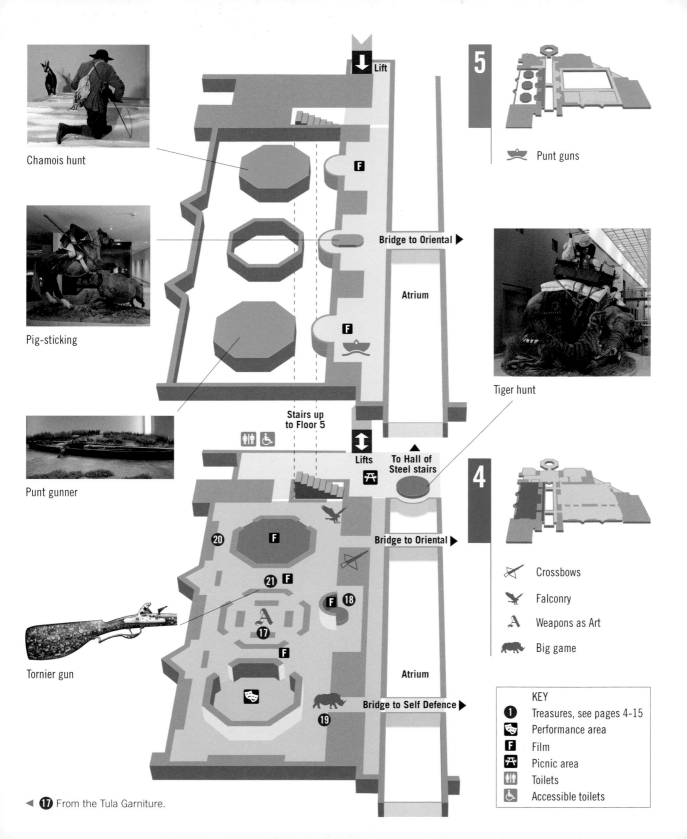

Chamois hunt

Pig-sticking

Punt gunner

Tornier gun

5

Punt guns

Tiger hunt

4

Crossbows

Falconry

Weapons as Art

Big game

Lift

F

Bridge to Oriental ▶

Atrium

**Stairs up
to Floor 5**

Lifts

**To Hall of
Steel stairs**

20 **F**

Bridge to Oriental ▶

21 **F**

F 18

17

F

19 **Bridge to Self Defence ▶**

Atrium

KEY

1 Treasures, see pages 4-15

Performance area

F Film

Picnic area

Toilets

Accessible toilets

◀ **17** From the Tula Garniture.

To many today hunting is repulsive and indefensible, to many it is right and natural, and to some it is still essential for survival. It is this story, both good and bad, which is told in this gallery. We also consider weapons as works of art, as the evidence of the pinnacle of a craftsman's skill.

Hunting weapons

Longbows

From prehistory bows were used to hunt game, and indeed are still in use in some countries today. However in England, where the longbow was such an important weapon of the armies of the Middle Ages, its use was restricted to the noble classes. Ordinary people, who were required by law to practise in its use for war, were strictly forbidden to hunt with it.

Crossbows

The longbow was a simple instrument but was only deadly in the hands of a skilled archer. By comparison a crossbow was a more complicated and expensive weapon, but required little skill to use. As it was slower to use than a longbow it was more suitable for siege defences and hunting rather than on the battlefield.

Crossbows are believed to have been invented by the Chinese in the 4th century BC. It was not until the 10th or 11th centuries AD that the crossbow became a military weapon in Europe. With the introduction of hand-held firearms it passed out of general military service in the 16th century but its use for hunting and target shooting has continued to the present day.

A crossbow is a projectile weapon which, depending on the type, shoots arrows, bolts, quarrels, stones or bullets. It consists of a bow attached crosswise to a stock called a tiller.

▼ English sporting crossbow with the stock inlaid with panels of staghorn and mother-of-pearl, in a style then popular in England and the Low Countries. XI.295

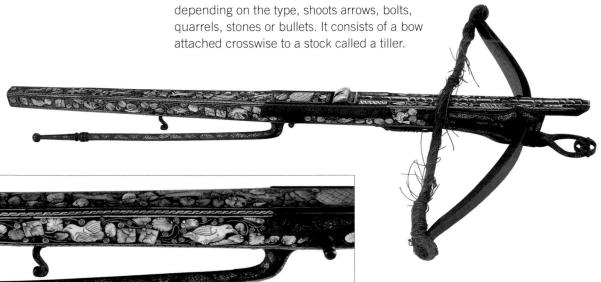

Whereas a longbow is used vertically the crossbow is used horizontally. The tiller is fitted with a trigger mechanism for the release of the bowstring. Early crossbows were spanned by hand but as technological developments made stronger bows possible they became more difficult to span this way and mechanisms were invented to overcome this. The result was that projectiles could be shot with greater force.

While the longbow remained plain and unadorned throughout its life, highly decorated crossbows became quite common by the 15th century.

Firearms

Firearms appeared in Europe in the early 14th century. The inaccuracy of these early guns, and the noise and smoke they produced, would have made them less successful than bows or crossbows as hunting weapons.

Improvements in gun making gradually made them more effective, however their use in hunting, until the end of the 17th century at least, was restricted to shooting at birds while they were at rest. Shooting at flying birds required an effective ignition system, and by around 1700 flintlock guns designed to shoot birds on the wing had been developed.

The flintlock always posed a problem for the sportsman, however, in that the puff of smoke from the priming powder was often seen by the bird at which he was shooting, giving the bird a brief but sufficient opportunity to 'jink', or turn suddenly, causing the charge of small lead shot to miss its mark.

Percussion ignition, invented in the early years of the 19th century by a keen Scottish sporting clergyman, the Reverend Alexander Forsyth, provided a major breakthrough in smokeless ignition, and is still the way by which almost all modern small arms cartridges are fired today.

▼ Top: Flintlock sporting gun. French, Alsace, dated 1646. The decoration of the stock inlaid with plain, yellow and green-stained stag horn, is of remarkable quality and was almost certainly by master craftsman Jean Conrad Tornier. XII.1549

▼ English sporting gun by John Shaw. A fine example of the type of long-barrelled gun which at the end of the 17th century became popular in much of Western Europe for shooting birds in flight. XII.5208

▲ Airgun with barrel reservoir, dated about 1740. XII.9556

Airguns

Airguns of considerable power and sophistication saw some use both militarily and for hunting, since the absence of powder smoke and their almost silent operation did not disturb the intended target or indeed others around it, whether human or animal. Rechargeable reservoirs containing compressed air allowed for a number of discharges, but the complexity and cost of such weapons meant that they did not achieve the widespread use of the more powerful, and less expensive, black-powder sporting guns.

Edged weapons

A number of different edged weapons were used in hunting, some depending upon which animal was the quarry. Boars and bears, which were both large and dangerous, were hunted with specially designed thrusting spears and swords. These weapons had crossbars which stopped the blade penetrating too deeply, which otherwise might not be easily withdrawn and, equally importantly, did not allow the wounded animal to slide up the blade and gore the hunter.

Once the animal had been killed the carcass would be butchered in preparation for the banquet that often followed such a grand social occasion. Some hunting swords had saw-back blades with which to dismember the kill. Special sets known as trousses included various choppers, bodkins, knives and forks, designed to be used for both the preparing and eating of the game.

Spears and swords for the chase were also very often heavily decorated, displaying both the owners' rank and wealth. Hunting hangers, for instance, which were shorter swords with a straight or slightly curved single-edged and pointed blade, and used for game such as deer, often had hilts made of precious materials such as ivory, cast bronze, semi-precious stone, or even porcelain. The blades themselves were often etched and gilded.

Falconry

Falconry is a hunting partnership between man and bird. The art is to cast the bird from your wrist into the sky from where it spies its prey, soars to its pitch and swoops down at speeds of up to 120 mph, killing the prey with a knock-out blow from its talons. It is one of the world's oldest sports and it is believed to have started in Mesopotamia over 4,000 years ago. In the Middle Ages it was a popular sport in Europe and an efficient way for catching small mammals and birds for the table. The introduction of firearms almost brought to an end the art of falconry – guns are more efficient weapons and do not need daily feeding and exercise!

▶ 'An Ugly Customer'. A recreation of an incident, described by H A Leveson, a Victorian big game hunter, in his book *Sport in Many Lands*, when he shot a tiger which attacked his elephant.

◀ Opposite left: Hunting hanger. The iron hilt is chiselled in the form of three dragons. IX.977

◀ Opposite: Hunting hanger made between 1650 and 1670. The cast and chased silver hilt is in the form of a lion being attacked by hounds. IX.849

Many objects in the Royal Armouries collection have a social relevance today - perhaps none more so than those in the Self Defence Gallery.

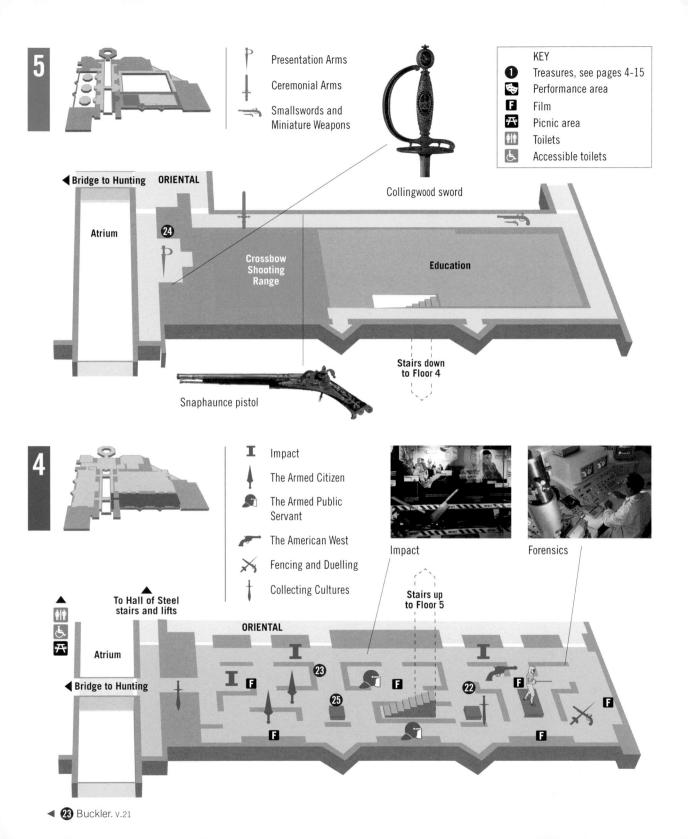

5

Presentation Arms

Ceremonial Arms

Smallswords and Miniature Weapons

Collingwood sword

◄ Bridge to Hunting ORIENTAL

KEY

1 Treasures, see pages 4-15

Performance area

F Film

Picnic area

Toilets

Accessible toilets

Atrium

24

Crossbow Shooting Range

Education

Stairs down to Floor 4

Snaphaunce pistol

4

I Impact

The Armed Citizen

The Armed Public Servant

The American West

Fencing and Duelling

Collecting Cultures

Impact

Forensics

Stairs up to Floor 5

To Hall of Steel stairs and lifts

ORIENTAL

Atrium

◄ Bridge to Hunting

23

25

22

Society has always tried to organise itself in various ways to control crimes of violence. The Self Defence Gallery displays explore this social history including gun crime in the local community and arms and armour in popular culture.

▼ Italian sword, dated 1490 – 1510. IX.1414

▼ European buckler (a small shield). V.47

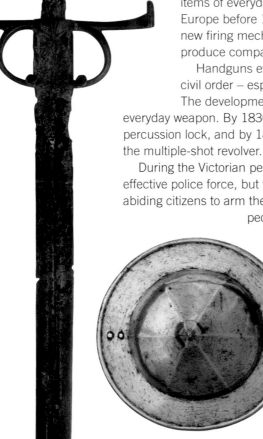

Self defence

In the Middle Ages very few people journeyed far from their homes. Roads in Britain and Europe were poor and there was a real danger of being attacked. With no organised police force to uphold the law, individuals had to protect themselves.

Travellers, traders and pilgrims armed themselves with daggers, swords and quarterstaffs. Civilians did not usually wear armour: it was expensive and most people would not have been able to afford much more than a small shield (buckler). For those who could afford it, a coat of mail, worn under the tunic, would have offered extra protection.

Most classes in society openly carried swords and daggers as items of everyday dress. Although primitive handguns appeared in Europe before 1400, it was not until the early 16th century that a new firing mechanism and improved gunpowder made it possible to produce compact guns ready to fire at the pull of a trigger.

Handguns eventually became common enough to be a threat to civil order – especially the pistol which could be easily concealed. The development of the flintlock by 1600 made the pistol a practical everyday weapon. By 1830 the flintlock had given way to the more reliable percussion lock, and by 1850 the single-shot weapon was often replaced by the multiple-shot revolver.

During the Victorian period crime was reduced, thanks to the increasingly effective police force, but fear of crime remained. It was common for law-abiding citizens to arm themselves with revolvers, pistols and knives. Some people carried more elegant concealed weapons such as the swordstick or the cane gun.

It was not until the 20th century that legal controls were introduced to limit the types of weapons which could be privately owned.

▶ Opposite: English rapier. IX.1494 A

▶ Opposite right: Italian ear dagger. The two flattened discs either side of the top of the grip give this group of daggers their name. X.258

▲ The American Henry rifle, the forerunner of the now legendary Winchester rifle. XII.2418

▲ Pinfire five-shot pepperbox, French. Made by Lefaucheux for the 1851 Great Exhibition held in London. XII.5297

Travel

Travelling the roads of England of the 17th and 18th century was a dangerous business as crime was rife. The growth of trade generated wealth and a travelling community. These traders and travellers represented rich pickings for the highwayman and footpad. There was no organised force to deter and detect crime. The country was served mostly by local constables and watch patrols who were often inefficient. In defence of their trade and profits, travellers armed themselves and their transport more heavily than before.

Travelling abroad

The coming of the industrial revolution in the 19th century and the invention of the railway and the steam train saw a rapid growth in the number of people travelling abroad. In this age of western imperialism more and more explorers, missionaries and hunters ventured out into uncharted regions across the globe.

Due the vast distances travelled much of the equipment needed had to be carried including not only the weapons for protection and hunting but also the means to repair them and to make ammunition. Small light engineering kits were developed incorporating extremely sophisticated and precise tools.

Civil forces

Public servants such as police and prison officers, Customs and Excise officers and Royal Mail coachmen were armed with a variety of weapons including edged weapons and firearms.

Mail coach guards

Poor roads made communication slow and difficult and post boys and coaches were often robbed. In 1784 a fast, well-protected nationwide system of coaches was set up. Every coach had a guard armed with a pair of flintlock pistols and a blunderbuss, which generally proved an effective defence.

The police

For many centuries law enforcement depended upon the local community. Magistrates appointed officers such as parish constables, who were unpaid, and watchmen to keep the peace.

In the 18th century, as towns expanded and population increased, this style of policing could not cope with the growing threats and fears of crime and disorder.

The first attempts at professional policing were made in London, and in 1829 the Metropolitan Police Force was established by Sir Robert Peel. It was not until 1856 that every local authority was required to have a police force.

With the Industrial Revolution and mass migration to the cities, law and order became increasingly important and a regular full-time paid force slowly developed.

The first police officers were armed with a wooden truncheon and sometimes a short sword. As firearms were increasingly used in crime the police were forced to respond by arming themselves and developing protective clothing.

◀ An interpretation of 'A Policeman's Lot'.

▶ Police truncheon, painted with the monogram of King George IV, 1820–30. VIII.160

Smuggling

By 1750 smuggling had become big business. There was a growing demand for luxury goods such as tobacco, tea, brandy and silks brought from overseas. As these were subject to heavy import duties, large profits were to be made smuggling them into the country. Naturally the government was anxious to reduce this loss of customs and excise revenue and instructed the Coastguard, backed by the army and Royal Navy, to patrol the coastal waters and inland roads. The smugglers were often well armed and pitched battles between smugglers and 'revenue men' were not uncommon.

▲ A brass-barrelled flintlock blunderbuss, fitted with a spring-operated bayonet. XII.1042

◄ Flintlock sea service pistol, an issue weapon to the Royal Navy during the Napoleonic Wars. XII.4554

◄ British police equipment: Police rattle, about 1840. XVIII.401

◄ Metropolitan helmet for use on a moped, after 1952. IV.1826

◄ Police truncheon, about 1950. XVIII.403

Fencing and duelling

Duelling was a way for 'gentlemen' to settle their quarrels. The duel of honour was fought in cold blood between gentlemen, one perhaps seeking 'satisfaction' from the other in response to an insult to his 'good name'.

Swords

At first personal combats were fought with a sword and a small shield (buckler). The rapier, a longer, narrower and more pointed sword used for thrusting was introduced after 1500. It often had an elaborate guard to protect the unarmoured hand. A new style of fencing developed, emphasising the use of the point instead of the edge of the blade.

▶ An illustration from *The School of Fencing* – a manual by the famous fencing master, Domenico Angelo (1765).

Swords were worn as part of a gentleman's everyday dress. One of the qualities thought to be desirable in a gentleman was his skill with a sword and there were many schools which taught the art of fencing. Although some students may have learned to use the sword with duelling in mind most considered it a sport. Schools of fencing, such as that in London of swordmaster Henry Angelo, became very popular.

Pistols

By about 1780 the pistol displaced the sword in the duel and many gentlemen owned a cased set of specialised duelling pistols. The duellist had to be able to aim and fire quickly and accurately, usually at a distance of not less than 15 m (50 feet).

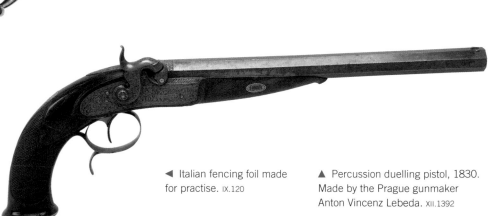

◀ Italian fencing foil made for practise. IX.120

▲ Percussion duelling pistol, 1830. Made by the Prague gunmaker Anton Vincenz Lebeda. XII.1392

Collecting Cultures

We encounter arms and armour on a regular basis in films, television, literature and art. These elaborate props and costumes inspire and intrigue us. Through our Collecting Cultures project, the Royal Armouries has explored the impact of the national collection of arms and armour using fantastic items of arms and armour made famous by popular culture. Among the items on display in the museum are the Lord of the Rings trilogy swords, James Bond firearms and a 'Vampire Killing Kit'.

▲ Centrefire self-loading pistol, a 'steampunk' movie prop from *The League of Extraordinary Gentlemen* (2003). XII.11938

▶ Sting: the sword of Frodo Baggins (2012). IX.5630

▶ Right: Orcrist, goblin cleaver: the sword of Thorin Oakenshield (2013). IX.5635

▼ Vampire killing kit. XII.11811

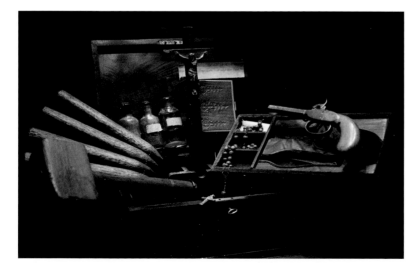

Visitor information

We aim to make your visit to the Royal Armouries as enjoyable as possible, and we offer a variety of ways for you to extend your experience both during and after your visit.

OPENING TIMES
Open daily, 10am – 5pm
(closed 24-26 December)

ENQUIRIES
For further information about Royal Armouries Leeds, please call 0113 220 1999, email enquiries@armouries.org.uk or visit www.royalarmouries.org

PARKING
CitiPark Leeds Dock is located a short walk from the museum with 1600 car parking spaces and bicycle storage available. Weekend discounts are often available.

ACCESSIBILITY
We aim to remove as many barriers to accessing our services as possible, and are constantly working towards improving and updating our facilities. For the most up-to-date accessibility information please visit our website or view our Euan's Guide pages at www.euansguide.com. Alternatively you can speak to a member of the team by calling 0113 220 1999.

EVENTS
Every day we run a varied programme of events ranging from talks and tours to performances and live combat demonstrations. We also have a regular series of special events, including our world-famous international jousting tournament, all designed to bring our unique collection of arms and armour to life. Please be aware that we occasionally demonstrate historic gun firing in our outdoor dockside amphitheatre using blank ammunition.

EDUCATION
Our dedicated education team runs a variety of hands-on, immersive workshops which use the world-class collection of the Royal Armouries to bring the school curriculum to life. For more information about this outstanding learning experience, email education@armouries.org.uk

PHOTOGRAPHY
You are welcome to take photographs and films at the museum for your personal use. Due to the fragility of many of the collection items, flash photography is prohibited in the galleries.

For commercial photography enquiries, please visit images.royalarmouries.org

LIBRARY AND ARCHIVE

We have one of the largest arms and armour reference libraries in the world, with special collections of early fencing books and military manuals, and an archive containing over 500,000 documents, files, photographs and films. Access is limited and by appointment only: please contact library@armouries.org.uk

CARING FOR OUR COLLECTION

Royal Armouries has an international reputation as a centre of excellence for the conservation and care of arms and armour. You may also see our expert teams of conservators and technicians at work in the galleries. Check the website for more information about our next maintenance week.

FOOD AND DRINK

You can enjoy seasonal home baking, freshly-made sandwiches, delicious hot snacks, crisp salads and a range of hot and cold drinks in one of our two catering outlets. Visit the café on the ground floor beside the main entrance or the coffee shop on the 2nd floor next to the lifts. No prior booking is required, but for further information (including dietary requirements) please call 0113 220 1906.

SHOPPING

The museum shop is located on the ground floor and stocks a carefully-curated range of exciting gifts and toys for all the family. Signed copies of Royal Armouries books as well as our collection of full-scale replica arms and armour are the perfect way to take history home with you. You can also browse online at shop.armouries.org

CROSSBOW RANGE

Take the gold lift to the fifth floor to test your skills on our crossbow range. You can purchase your bolts at reception or at the range.

MEETINGS AND CONFERENCES

New Dock Hall can provide an idyllic setting for your next event. From 20 to 1500 delegates, we can deliver conferences, banquets, exhibitions and weddings, and will be delighted to coordinate every aspect of your event from initial planning to your transport home. Full details and venue plans can be found at www.rai-events.co.uk

SUPPORT US

We rely on your support. As a charity, every pound donated is invested back into the museum, helping us to care for our collections and keep admission free for everyone. Thank you for your generosity.

ABOUT THE ROYAL ARMOURIES

The Royal Armouries is the United Kingdom's national museum of arms and armour, and one of the most important museums of its type in the world.

We have a long history, dating from the Middle Ages. Our celebrated core collection originated in the nation's working arsenal, which was assembled over many centuries at the Tower of London. The fact that objects were displayed to the public in Queen Elizabeth I's reign (1558-1603) makes us heir to one of the first deliberately devised visitor attractions in the country.

Our collection of about 75,000 items – excluding approximately 2,700 loans to other bodies – is now displayed and housed in our historic home at the White Tower in the Tower of London but also at our purpose-built museum in Leeds, and at Fort Nelson. Together these three sites attract over two million visitors every year.

In 2005 the museum acquired the former Ministry of Defence Pattern Room reference collection, originally started to govern the manufacture of military arms and armour. This collection began at the Tower of London, like that of the Royal Armouries, but then moved to the Royal Small Arms Factory at Enfield. The bulk of it is now housed at the National Firearms Centre, Leeds.

To find out more about our work, please visit www.royalarmouries.org

Front cover: Elephant Armour, xxvia.16, 23, 102 a-f, 259; xxvii.218; xxvim.6; al.290 105. Image courtesy of Charlotte Graham Photography (www.charlottegraham.photography).

Front cover flap: The 'Horned Helmet'. iv.22

Pages 70-71: Events, collection care images courtesy of Charlotte Graham Photography.

Inside back cover: Jousting tournament in the Royal Armouries tiltyard. Image courtesy of Claire Bilyard.

Back cover: Royal Armouries Museum, Leeds Dock. Quote: Act I, Scene I, *Richard III,* by William Shakespeare.

Published by Royal Armouries Museum, Armouries Drive, Leeds LS10 1LT, United Kingdom

www.royalarmouries.org

Copyright © 2019 Trustees of the Royal Armouries

ISBN 978 0 94809 298 5

Edited by Martyn Lawrence

Designed by Geraldine Mead

Maps by Graham Moores

Object photography by Gary Ombler, Jacob Bishop

Interpretation photography by Steve Gabbett

Printed by W&G Baird

10 9 8 7 6 5 4 3 2 1

A CIP record for this book is available from the British Library